AF507434

Published in the United States of America.

Volume I, Edition 1, First Publishing, 2020

Illustration by Evgenia Vernadskaya.

Book design and Recipes by Sunny Payne.

ISBN: 979-8-5783-1410-0

Sunny Payne Publishing

www.SunnyPayne.com

Sunny Payne's 3-Day Alkaline Vegan Meal Guide
(Soy-Free + Gluten-Free!)

Eating alkaline involves eating lots of plant-based foods and avoiding consuming items that cause acids to form in the body when you ingest them. Acids form when you eat or drink things that your body has to work harder (by producing more acid) to digest. These foods include cooked tomatoes or tomato sauce, coffee, refined or processed grains like white rice, bread and cereal, and sugary foods or drinks like soda and candy. Acids form in the body every time you consume meat, eggs and dairy as well.

The results of eating a lot of acid-forming foods can be gas, acid reflux, gastrointestinal discomfort, bloating, fatigue, inflammation, weight gain, and/or acidosis to name a few. It is my opinion that the actual number of ailments associated with acid forming diets is inumerable.

Alkaline foods include whole foods like fruits and vegetables, unprocessed grains, beans and legumes. Committing to an alkaline diet means your body expends less energy in the digestive process because you're eating foods that are easy to digest - this can help with weight regulation and will lead to the whole body feeling better and more energetic!

This short e-book shares some yummy recipes that I enjoy making! Breakfast, lunch and dinner meals for 3 days are included, along with two guilt-free desserts. Enjoy!

Day 1

Tapioca Crepes + Berry Compote

Prep time: 20 min   Cook time: 10 min   Serves: 4

Crepe Ingredients

- ¾ cup tapioca flour
- ¼ cup flaxseed meal
- ½ cup warm water
- ½ cup coconut mylk
- 1 teaspoon vanilla extract
- ¼ teaspoon salt
- 2 tablespoons of oil to coat frying pan

Berry Compote Ingredients

- 1 cup fresh or frozen organic berries
- 3 tablespoons filtered water
- 1/4 cup organic coconut sugar
- 1 tablespoon cornstarch + more if needed
- 1 tablespoon fresh-squeezed lemon juice
- 1 teaspoon ground cinnamon
- 1 teaspoon vanilla extract

Instructions

1. In a small bowl, whisk together the flaxseed meal and ½ cup of warm water. Let this sit for 10 minutes to thicken and create the flegg, or egg-substitute
2. Make the berry compote by combining all compote ingredients in a small saucepan on the stove over medium heat
3. Whisk the berry mixture so there are no lumps from the cornstarch and allow the mixture to heat up and bubble
4. In a large mixing bowl combine tapioca flour and salt
5. Whisk flegg and vanilla into the batter and add the coconut mylk 1 tablespoon at a time until the batter has no lumps and is slightly runny
6. Heat a skillet over medium-high heat and coat with oil
7. Pour ¼ of the batter into the pan in a thin layer and in a large circle
8. Cook on one side for 1 to 2 minutes, then flip and cook the other side for 45 seconds or until the batter seems completely done
9. Stir the compote occasionally, letting it bubble and let the berries cook down
10. Put batter on a plate and cook the rest in the same way until you have 4, stacking the crepes on top of each other to keep them warm
11. When you are finished cooking the crepes, layer the fruit compote in the middle and roll, then enjoy!

Cauliflower Tabbouleh Salad

Prep time: 20 min   Cook time: 5 min   Serves: 4

Ingredients

- 1 head of cauliflower
- 4 cups salad greens
- 12 cherry tomatoes
- 1 small red onion
- 2 cucumbers
- ¼ cup olive oil
- 3 tablespoons fresh-squeezed lemon juice
- 1 teaspoon pink salt
- 1 teaspoon ground black pepper
- 1 teaspoon cumin
- ¼ cup fresh parsley
- ¼ cup fresh cilantro
- ¼ cup fresh mint

Instructions

1. Get cauliflower into rice-like consistency by chopping and then pulsing in a food processor or high-speed blender
2. Chop and seed tomatoes, dice onions and cucumber, chop herbs
3. Combine all ingredients Tand enjoy this salad over your favorite salad greens (I like baby spinach and arugula!)

Raw Vegetable Chips

Prep time: 15 min   Cook time: 0 min   Serves: 4

Ingredients

- 2 large carrots
- 2 large cucumbers
- 1 teaspoon pink salt
- 1 teaspoon ground black pepper
- 1 teaspoon garlic powder

Instructions

1. Slice carrots and cucumbers into rounds about 1-centimeter thick (chip size)
2. Sprinkle a tiny amount of salt, pepper and garlic powder on each round
3. Enjoy this simple raw snack!

Lentil Stuffed Potato Pockets

Prep time: 20 min   Cook time: 45 min   Serves: 4

Dough Ingredients

- 2 pounds of potatoes
- ½ cup oat flour
- ⅓ cup tapioca flour or cornstarch
- ½ teaspoon himalayan salt
- ½ teaspoon ground black pepper

Filling Ingredients

- ¾ cup green lentils, rinsed and sorted
- 2 cups vegetable broth
- 1 cup mushrooms
- 1 bell pepper
- 1 large red onion
- 3 cloves of garlic
- 1 teaspoon cumin
- 1 teaspoon smoked paprika
- 1 teaspoon turmeric
- 1 teaspoon coriander powder
- ½ teaspoon pink salt
- ½ teaspoon ground black pepper
- 1 bay leaf
- 3 tablespoons sunflower oil

Instructions

1. Peel and chop the potatoes then boil them in water with salt added for 20 minutes until tender
2. Chop mushrooms, pepper, onion and garlic
3. Heat sunflower oil in a separate pot over medium high heat, saute mushrooms for 3 minutes then add pepper and onions and saute for 3 minutes, add garlic and saute for one minute
4. Add the broth, lentils, spices, and bay leaf and bring to a boil. Cover with a lid after boiling, lower heat to simmer, cook for 25 minutes
5. When the potatoes are done boiling, drain the water then use a fork or potato masher to mash all the potatoes with pepper
6. When the potatoes cool down, add gluten-free flour and cornstarch, mix well to make the dough
7. Separate the dough into 8 pieces to be used for the potato pockets. Flatten each dough piece into a 1 cm thick circle
8. When the lentils are finished cooking, place a scoop onto one half of each dough round and fold the other half over, pressing the edges together
9. Heat sunflower oil over medium-high heat and fry the potato pockets on each side for 3 minutes or until golden brown, then enjoy

Watermelon Lime Sorbet

Prep time: 10 min   Cook time: 5 min   Serves: 4

Ingredients

- 1 whole watermelon
- 3 limes, juiced
- 1 cup of ice + more if necessary

Instructions

1. Cut all fruit from watermelon and add to a blender
2. Juice the limes and add the juice, removing any seeds
3. Add ice ½ a cup at a time and blend until smooth and thick
4. Enjoy right after blending, or put the sorbet in a bowl and cover and freeze for at least one hour to enjoy extra cold!

Day 2

Peaches n' Cream Smoothie

Prep time: 5 min   Cook time: 2 min   Serves: 4

Ingredients

- 3 ripe peaches
- 2 bananas
- 1 cup fresh strawberries
- 1 cup oat or coconut mylk
- ¼ cup orange or lemon juice
- 2 tablespoons chia seeds
- 6 ice cubes

Instructions

1. Peel bananas, pit peaches and add all ingredients except ice to the blender
2. Pulse until smooth, adding ice as desired
3. Enjoy!

Potato Hash Skillet

Prep time: 15 min   Cook time: 25 min   Serves: 4

Ingredients

- 2 large potatoes
- 1 large sweet potato
- 4 large carrots
- 8 ounces of shiitake mushrooms
- 2 cups chopped kale
- 1 bell pepper
- 1 large white onion
- 2 cloves of garlic
- 3 tablespoons extra virgin olive oil
- 1 teaspoon dried cilantro
- 1 teaspoon cumin
- 1 teaspoon chili powder
- ½ teaspoon smoked paprika
- ½ teaspoon red pepper flakes
- 2 cups cooked black or pinto beans
- 2 teaspoons fresh-squeezed lime juice

Instructions

1. Chop the potatoes, carrots and sweet potato into small bite-sized pieces, slice the mushrooms, peppers and onions into strips, and mince the garlic
2. Remove kale from stems and chop into bite-sized pieces
3. Heat olive oil over medium heat in a medium cast-iron skillet
4. Add potatoes to the skillet and cook for 10-12 minutes, stirring occasionally. Add more oil if needed
5. Add mushrooms and turn the heat to medium-high. Saute for another 3 minutes
6. Add kale and saute for 3 minutes.
7. Turn heat to medium-high, then add the peppers and onions and saute for 3 more minutes
8. Add the garlic, cilantro, cumin, smoked paprika, red pepper flakes, and chili powder and saute for one minute
9. Add the beans and mix together until heated through, about 3 minutes then drizzle fresh lime juice on top, turn off heat & enjoy!

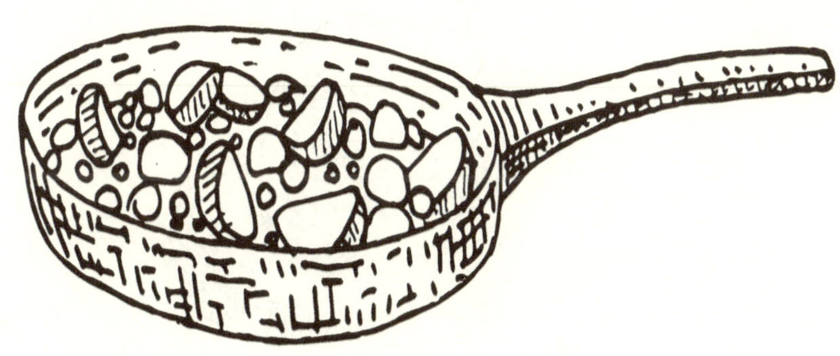

Lentil and Quinoa Stuffed Peppers

Prep time: 20 min   Cook time: 55 min   Serves: 4

<u>Ingredients</u>

- 4 large red, yellow, or orange bell peppers
- ¾ cup green lentils, rinsed and sorted
- ¾ cup red quinoa, rinsed
- 3 ½ cups vegetable broth
- 1 red onion
- 3 cloves garlic
- 1 bay leaf
- 1 teaspoon cumin
- 1 teaspoon black pepper
- 1 teaspoon smoked paprika
- ½ teaspoon pink salt
- 3 tablespoons sunflower oil
- 2 sliced avocados
- 1 bunch of fresh cilantro
- Vegan cheeze for topping (optional)

Instructions

1. Preheat oven to 375 degrees Fahrenheit (190 Celsius)
2. Chop the red onion and mince the garlic
3. Heat sunflower oil in a medium pot with a lid over medium-high heat
4. Add the onions to the pot and saute for 3 minutes, then add garlic to the pot and saute for 1 additional minute
5. Add vegetable broth, lentils, cumin, pepper, paprika, salt, and the bay leaf to the pot and bring to a boil
6. After boiling, turn heat down to simmer, cover the pot with a lid, and cook lentils for 15 minutes. After 15 minutes, add rinsed and drained quinoa and cook for another 15 minutes until lentils and quinoa are tender
7. While the lentils cook, wash and prepare the peppers. Cut them in half, remove and discard the stem and all seeds. Wash the inside of the peppers well
8. Oil a baking tray and place pepper halves on the tray, with the cut side up
9. When the lentils finish cooking, scoop lentils into peppers so that they are stuffed. Bake for 10 minutes then cover with foil and bake for an additional 15 minutes then remove from the oven, let cool and enjoy!

Tip: Add vegan cheeze to melt on top for the last 15 minutes of baking, top with fresh cilantro and sliced avocado to serve.

Kale and Onions

Prep time: 5 min   Cook time: 10 min   Serves: 4

Ingredients

- 3 tablespoons extra virgin olive oil
- 1 small red onion, cut in thin strips
- 1 bunch of kale, leaves pulled off stems and chopped
- 2 cloves of garlic, minced
- 3 tablespoons sunflower oil
- ½ teaspoon pink salt
- ½ teaspoon ground black pepper

Instructions

1. Heat sunflower oil in a large cast-iron skillet over medium-high heat
2. Check the temperature of the oil by flicking a drop of water into the skillet. When the water drops start to sizzle, add all of the kale at once
3. Stir kale while cooking for 3 minutes. Then season with salt and pepper
4. Add onions to the skillet and saute for 4-5 minutes
5. Add garlic to the skillet and saute for another minute. The kale leaves should start to turn crispy on the curly edges. Enjoy as a side for any meal!

Banana Nice Cream

Ingredients

- 5 ripe bananas
- 1 ripe mango
- ½ cup cashew or coconut mylk
- 1 avocado
- 1 tablespoon maple syrup

Instructions

1. Peel fruit, seed the mango and avocado
2. Blend all ingredients until smooth (add more mylk if necessary for a smooth and thick consistency)
3. Put nice cream in a bowl and cover, freeze 4-6 hours
4. Enjoy creamy and cold!

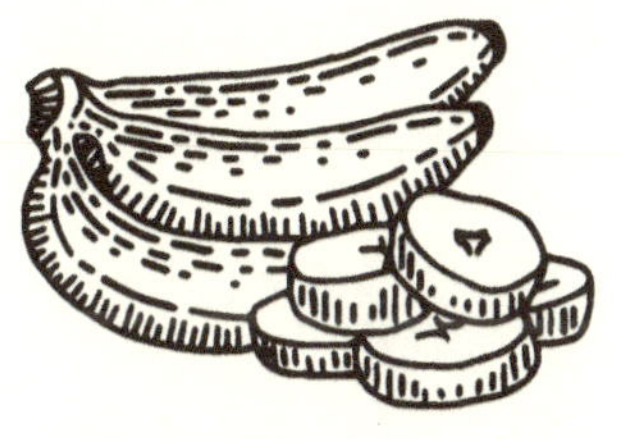

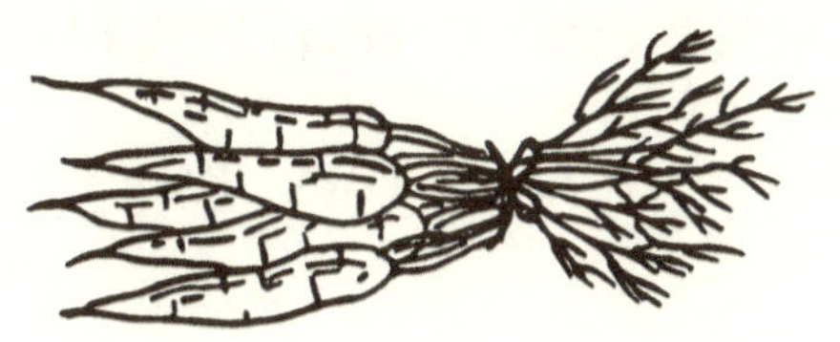

Day 3

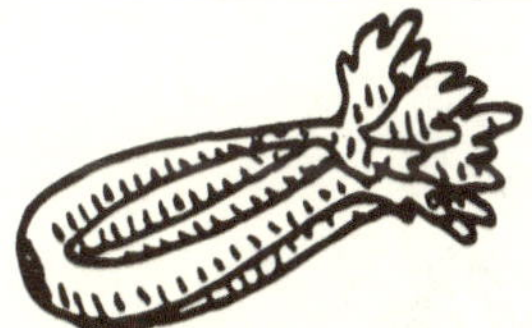

Chickpea Flour Omelette

Prep time: 15 min   Cook time: 20 min   Serves: 4

<u>Omelette Batter Ingredients</u>

- 1 cup chickpea flour
- 1 ⅓ cups water (or vegetable broth for more flavor)
- ¼ cup nutritional yeast
- 1 teaspoon garlic powder
- 1 teaspoon onion powder
- ½ teaspoon baking soda
- ¼ teaspoon turmeric
- ¼ teaspoon pink salt
- ¼ teaspoon ground black pepper

<u>Filling Ingredients</u>

- 2 tablespoons sunflower oil + more if necessary
- ½ a red onion, diced
- 1 red bell pepper, diced
- 8 ounces mushrooms, diced
- 2 cups fresh baby spinach leaves
- 2 cloves garlic, minced

Instructions

1. Mix all batter ingredients in a large mixing bowl and combine until smooth
2. Heat frying pan on the stove over medium-high heat with 2 tablespoons of sunflower oil
3. Add diced mushrooms and cook for 3 minutes, add bell pepper and cook for 2 minutes, add onions and spinach and cook for 3-4 minutes until the spinach is wilted, then remove the pan from the heat and transfer vegetables to a bowl
4. In the same frying pan, add another 2 tablespoons of oil and heat over medium-high heat
5. Add ¼ of the batter to the pan and cook for 5-7 minutes, until the mixture begins bubbling
6. Add ¼ of the cooked vegetables and flip the omelette over to cook the other side for another 3-5 minutes
7. After 5 minutes of cooking, toss fresh cilantro on the omelette and fold in half
8. Repeat additional omelettes until all the batter and vegetables are cooked
9. Enjoy!

Tip: Making your own chickpea flour is a great option if you have a high-speed food processor, as buying dried chickpeas in bulk is fairly cheap at health food stores.

Green Bean Salad

Prep time: **15** min   Cook time: **10** min   Serves: 4

Salad Ingredients

- 4 cups fresh salad greens
- 1 cup green beans or snap peas
- ½ cup slivered almonds
- 2 large carrots, chopped
- ½ cup of hemp seeds and dried cranberries

Lemon Tahini Dressing Ingredients

- 1 cup tahini
- ¼ cup to ½ cup filtered water
- 3 tablespoons fresh-squeezed lemon juice
- ½ teaspoon pink himalayan salt
- ½ teaspoon ground black pepper
- ½ teaspoon paprika
- ½ teaspoon cumin

Instructions

1. Blend all dressing ingredients until smooth
2. For a thinner dressing, add water 1 tbsp at a time until you reach desired consistency
3. Combine salad ingredients and enjoy with this dressing!

Blueberry Banana Smoothie

Prep time: 5 min   Cook time: 1 min   Serves: 4

Ingredients

- 2 ripe bananas
- 2 cups fresh blueberries
- 2 cups coconut mylk or cashew mylk
- 1 cup ice
- ¼ cup peanut butter
- 2 tablespoons hemp seeds

Instructions

1. Blend all ingredients with half the ice
2. Add the rest of the ice ¼ cup at a time until the smoothie is your desired consistency
3. Enjoy on its own or as a smoothie bowl topped with fresh sliced strawberries and chia seeds!

One-Pot Pumpkin Soup

Prep time: 15 min   Cook time: 55 min   Serves: 6

Ingredients

- 1 medium pumpkin, scooped and seeded
- 2 cups cooked white beans
- 2 large sweet potatoes
- 1 medium white onion
- 2 sticks of celery
- 3 large carrots
- 3 garlic cloves
- ¼ cup fresh rosemary
- ¼ cup fresh basil
- ¼ fresh thyme
- ¼ cup fresh oregano
- 2 bay leaves
- 1 teaspoon pink salt
- 1 teaspoon ground black pepper
- ½ teaspoon paprika
- 3 tablespoons extra virgin olive oil
- 6 cups vegetable broth

Instructions

1. Chop pumpkin, sweet potatoes and carrots into small bite-sized pieces
2. Chop onions and celery very fine and mince garlic
3. Heat olive oil in a large pot over medium heat
4. Add diced carrots, pumpkin and sweet potatoes, stir for 5 minutes
5. Add onion and celery, stir for 2 minutes
6. Add garlic and herbs, stir for 2 minutes
7. Add vegetable broth, cooked white beans, spices, fresh chopped herbs and bay leaf
8. Cover and cook on simmer for 30 to 40 minutes until pumpkin is tender
9. Enjoy served with fresh rosemary sprig on top, served with gluten-free crackers or rice cakes!

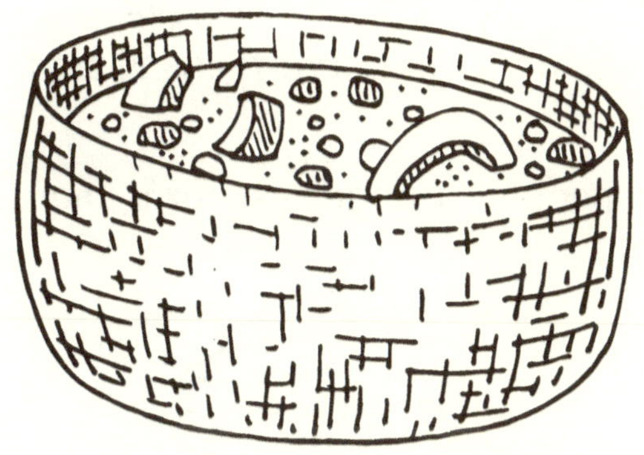

Avocado Chocolate Pudding

Ingredients

- 3 medium-sized ripe avocados
- 2 tablespoons of hemp seeds
- 4 tablespoons cocoa powder
- 1 teaspoon vanilla extract
- 1 tablespoon agave
- 1 tablespoon lemon juice
- ¼ teaspoon pink himalayan salt
- 1 cup coconut mylk + more if necessary

Instructions

1. Blend until smooth, add extra mylk for desired consistency
2. Chill at least 1 hour before serving
3. Enjoy alone or with gluten-free graham crackers

Tip: Add 1 teaspoon of orange zest for a chocolate-orange flavored treat!

Thank you!

Other titles by Sunny include:

9 798578 314100